# a Minute for Mommy

# a Minute for
# Mommy

Reflecting on the
Blessings of Motherhood

Berkli Binns

TATE PUBLISHING & *Enterprises*

*a Minute for Mommy*
Copyright © 2010 by Berkli Binns. All rights reserved.

No part of this publication may be reproduced, stored in a retrieval system or transmitted in any way by any means, electronic, mechanical, photocopy, recording or otherwise without the prior permission of the author except as provided by USA copyright law.

Scripture quotations marked (KJV) are taken from the Holy Bible, King James Version, Cambridge, 1769. Used by permission. All rights reserved.

Scripture quotations marked (NASB) are taken from the New American Standard Bible®, Copyright © 1960, 1962, 1963, 1968, 1971, 1972, 1973, 1975, 1977, 1995 by The Lockman Foundation. Used by permission.

Scripture quotations marked (NIV) are taken from the Holy Bible, New International Version®. NIV®. Copyright© 1973, 1978, 1984 by International Bible Society. Used by permission of Zondervan. All rights reserved.

Scripture quotations marked (NKJV) are taken from the New King James Version®. Copyright © 1982 by Thomas Nelson, Inc. Used by permission. All rights reserved.

Scripture quotations marked (NLT) are taken from the Holy Bible, New Living Translation, copyright © 1996. Used by permission of Tyndale House Publishers, Inc., Wheaton, Illinois 60189. All rights reserved.

The opinions expressed by the author are not necessarily those of Tate Publishing, LLC.

Published by Tate Publishing & Enterprises, LLC
127 E. Trade Center Terrace | Mustang, Oklahoma 73064 USA
1.888.361.9473 | www.tatepublishing.com

Tate Publishing is committed to excellence in the publishing industry. The company reflects the philosophy established by the founders, based on Psalm 68:11,
*"The Lord gave the word and great was the company of those who published it."*

Book design copyright © 2010 by Tate Publishing, LLC. All rights reserved.
*Cover design by Blake Brasor*
*Interior design by Joey Garrett*

Published in the United States of America

ISBN: 978-1-61663-965-5
Family & Relationships / Parenting / Motherhood
10.08.30

# Dedication

To Richard, you are the love of my life
and my greatest encourager.

To Clay and Caleb, you inspire me and
fill me with immeasurable joy.

Delight yourself in the Lord and he will give you
the desires of your heart.

Psalm 37:4 (NIV)

# Acknowledgments

- My Lord and Savior and the director of my path, thank you so much for blessing me with my two precious little boys and for teaching me through my experience with them more about your unconditional love every day. This book would not have been possible without you.

- Richard, from the first time I mentioned my dream of writing a book, you believed in me. When this dream started to become a reality, you were ready and available to help me without hesitation. Thank you for your willingness to take care of the boys on many evenings and Sunday afternoons while I wrote the pages of these stories. I could never have done this without you. Your love and support means more to me than you will ever know. I love you with all my heart.

- Clay and Caleb, my love for you both is deeper than you could ever know. You bring so much joy to my life. I am so grateful God has allowed me to be your mom. Thank you for being the inspiration behind this book. I pray you will feel my deep love for you when you are old enough to read it.

  - Clay, I love your amazing energy and the way you truly embrace life. You are very creative and you make me laugh—a lot. You are always willing and ready to offer a helping hand. You have melted my heart from the sound of your first cry. You are such a joy to me.

- Little Bubba Lee, I appreciate and admire your sweet and loving spirit. You have a smile that lights up a room. At the tender age of three, I can already tell you have a servant's heart. You make me feel very special. I have seen God work many miracles in your young life, and I am forever grateful. Thank you both for making me smile every day. I love you dearly.

- To my family—the Wooldridges, Purcells, and Binns—I never could have asked for more wonderful family members. Each and every one of you has touched my heart in a special way. Whether I was born into your family or married into it, I have felt complete acceptance. Thank you so much for always being there for me, for supporting me, for teaching me, for guiding me, and for loving me so unconditionally. I am forever grateful. I love each of you so very much.

- To my church family, a very special thank you to my First Baptist Church of Bentonville family. I am amazed by your deep commitment to the Lord and dedicated care for the people not only in our congregation but in our community. I am constantly challenged to strengthen my walk with the Lord. I am especially thankful for each member of my Impact Sunday school class. Each of you holds a special place in my heart. I am also grateful for my former Sunday school class and its teachers, Jason and Michelle Nichol. Jason, I can never thank you enough for your part in leading me to the Lord. Michelle, your faithfulness in your own walk with the Lord and dedication to listening to the needs of others has touched me deeply. I could never ask for a greater church home.

- My faithful friends:

  - Sarah Vizena, what would I do without you? Thank you so much for taking time out of your busy schedule to proofread my manuscript. I appreciate your feedback and suggestions more than you know. More importantly, thank you for being my friend. I know I can count on you to be there when I need you. I will always be there for you too. You are a very special person.

  - Rachel Sargent, Sabrina Rampy, Shelli Rushing, and Danielle Shasteen, God blessed me so much when he introduced me to the four of you during my first couple of years in Bentonville. I never dreamed how deep our friendship would grow. We have shared Bible study time, coffee chats, birthday lunches, and, most importantly, friendship. Thank you for believing in me and for helping me believe in myself. I treasure you all so much.

  - Amy Arnott, Claire Reeves, and Jennifer Turner, we have known each other for many years. Thank you for being faithful friends, regardless of where our paths have taken us. You all are always on my side, and I love the way you always make me laugh and smile when I really need it. We have a bond that cannot be broken.

- To my blog followers, especially Laurie Orman, whose suggestion to turn my stories into a book gave me confidence that my dream could become a reality. I pray this book encourages you all.

- To Dr. Carol Reeves, thank you for the many purple pen marks on the pages of my college papers. I never could have succeeded or believed in myself as a writer without your teaching and guidance. You were more than a teacher to me; you were a mentor. I appreciate you so much.

- To the girls in my Dallas Bible study groups, I loved our precious time studying God's Word together. It was during this time in my life my desire to study God's Word and seek God's plan really grew. Even though many of us have relocated, I know we all care deeply for each other. You are friends I will never forget. Thank you all for the special impact you made on my life.

- To the associates at Panera in Bentonville, Arkansas, I never could have finished my manuscript without your friendly service and amazing atmosphere. Thank you for your encouragement and kindness during my writing process.

- To the entire staff at Tate Publishing, especially my acquisitions representative, Donna Chumley, and my editor, Callie Ferguson, thank you for making my dream of becoming an author a reality. You are an amazing group of people to work with. I am so thankful God guided me to your God-centered company. I cannot thank each of you enough.

For nothing is impossible with God.

Luke 1:37 (NIV)

# Table of Contents

Preface . . . . . . . . . . . . . . . . . . 13
Introduction . . . . . . . . . . . . . . . 15

**Thirty-one Daily Devotionals** . . . . . . . . . . . **19**
   Thank Goodness for Microwaves . . . . . . 21
   A Kiss a Day Keeps the Doctor Away . . . . 23
   You Can Do It. . . . . . . . . . . . . . . . 25
   The Blessing of Friendship . . . . . . . . . 27
   Been on a Date Lately? . . . . . . . . . . . 29
   God's Peace Is Waiting for You . . . . . . . 32
   You Know You Are a Mom When… . . . . 34
   Yes, Mommy Makes Mistakes Too . . . . . 37
   Jesus Took the Nails . . . . . . . . . . . . 40
   Creativity Equals Chaos . . . . . . . . . . 43
   You Can Admit It. You Are Tired. . . . . . 46
   Do I Really Have to Leave the Hospital? . . 49
   Searching for God . . . . . . . . . . . . . 52
   Because It Makes You Happy . . . . . . . 54
   So Proud of Me? . . . . . . . . . . . . . . 56

Have You Seen My Hurt, Dada? . . . . . . . 59
Someday, When I Get Bigger . . . . . . . . 62
I Know Where You Are . . . . . . . . . . 65
Following the Leader . . . . . . . . . . . 67
Can We Have a Mommy Day Today? . . . . 70
Momma, I Love You . . . . . . . . . . . . 73
I Love Room Check . . . . . . . . . . . . 75
Where's the Pink? . . . . . . . . . . . . . 78
Momma, Momma—Airplane! . . . . . . . 81
Full Speed Ahead . . . . . . . . . . . . . 83
Waiting at the Window . . . . . . . . . . 86
Don't Miss Out . . . . . . . . . . . . . . 89
Celebrate the "Ahhh" Moments . . . . . . 92
No Matter What . . . . . . . . . . . 94
I Will Fight the Giant . . . . . . . . . . . 97
A Minute for You . . . . . . . . . . . . 100

**They Make Me Smile Journal** . . . . . . . . . 103

**Prayer and Praises to Our Lord Journal** . . . . 119
Final Thoughts . . . . . . . . . . . . . . . 135

Behold, children are a gift of the Lord, The fruit of the womb is a reward.

Psalm 127:3 (NASB)

# Preface

Dear reader,

Writing this book took me on a journey far more exciting than I ever imagined. I traveled back in time to the beautiful sound of my son's first cry. I reminisced over sleepless nights, special "first" moments, and funny sayings. I climbed mountains of joy, and I paused in valleys where I shed many tears. I laughed. I rejoiced. I was greatly humbled.

God used the writing of this book to encourage me, give me hope, and to remind me how blessed I am to be a mom. He reminded me I am not alone on this journey of motherhood. The Lord has been with me every step of the way, and he will never leave me.

The stories on the pages of this book remind me that as much as I love my precious children, my Lord and Savior loves me even more. My hope is for every reader of this book to find themselves on their own special journey where, as they reflect on the blessing of motherhood, they are drawn into a closer relationship with their children and, most importantly, their Lord.

I hope this book will be a keepsake for you and your children for years to come.

Trust in the Lord with all your heart and do not lean on your own understanding. In all your ways acknowledge him, and he will make your paths straight.

Proverbs 3:5–6 (NASB)

# Introduction

I am so excited you have opened the pages of this devotional. As the mother of two young children, I understand how difficult it is to find time to take a hot shower, much less read a book. However, I also recognize the importance of taking a few minutes each day to rest and recharge. This book is divided into three sections, each designed to encourage you and give you comfort and peace—something every mother needs. Because your time is precious, this book was also designed to take only a few minutes of your time each day.

## Thirty-one Daily Devotionals

The book begins with a collection of thirty-one short stories inspired by my motherhood experiences. You may choose to complete it in a month or just pick it up when you need a little bit of encouragement. Either way, in order to gain the most out of it, I recommend you read only one story per day and reflect on the remarkable impact your children have on your life and your walk with God. At the end of each story is a section called "Take Just a Minute." Use this space to write any special reflections, action steps, or notes on how the Lord spoke to you. You may also want to use this space to write out a prayer to your heavenly Father. I want to encourage you to pray through these short stories and allow God to encourage you and guide you. The most important part of this book is not what I have written on the pages, but what I hope you will gain as you reflect on them.

## They Make Me Smile Journal

As the short stories of this book are read, I hope moms will recall special times with their own little ones. This section is for capturing these memories. Journaling has always been a very important part of my life. I don't want to forget any funny, silly, and serious moments. Writing down the memorable actions and sayings of your children is an excellent way to remember the past and a wonderful resource for laughter when the tough times occur. Your children will also enjoy reading about themselves when they get older. I hope you will continue to journal the moments that make you smile long after the pages provided for you in this book are full.

## Prayer and Praises to Our Lord Journal

The final section of this book will be for entering prayer requests and praises as they relate to raising children. I believe prayer is an essential part of a mother's life. Reaching out to our Lord is the most important action you can take. I hope the stories in this book encourage the reader to call out to the Lord for guidance, strength, and direction and, most importantly, to give praise to our King. I hope these journal pages will become a regular reference tool and a great stepping stone for keeping a prayer journal for years to come.

> "Call to me and I will answer you, and I will tell you great and mighty things, which you do not know."
>
> Jeremiah 33:3 (NASB)

# Thirty-one Daily Devotionals

## Reflecting on the Blessings of Motherhood

He called a little child and had him stand among them. And he said: "I tell you the truth, unless you change and become like little children, you will never enter the kingdom of heaven. Therefore, whoever humbles himself like this child is the greatest in the kingdom of heaven.

Matthew 18:2–4 (NIV)

# Thank Goodness for Microwaves

When I wake up in the morning, I cannot wait to pour myself a cup of coffee. I have dreams of sitting down in my favorite chair, taking in the quiet of the morning, and enjoying every last sip. Unfortunately, just as I pour that beautiful cup of coffee, I often hear someone yell, "Mommy, I need you!" No more fresh coffee. No more favorite chair. No more quiet morning. My coffee will have to wait. Thank goodness for microwaves.

As a mom, we feel tired and overwhelmed at times. We long for a few moments to sit and relax. We love and adore our children, but from time to time, we feel worn out and weary. We feel alone.

Be encouraged, you are not alone. God is there beside you and will help you along the way. Reach out to him. Pray to God each morning when you wake up. Ask him to be your caffeine. He will lift you up when you are down. He will give you hope when you are discouraged. He will give you energy when you need strength. God will recharge you more than a cup of coffee any day.

Yet those who wait for the Lord will gain new strength; they will mount up with wings like eagles, They will run and not get tired, They will walk and not become weary.

Isaiah 40:31 (NASB)

## Take Just a Minute

# A Kiss a Day Keeps the Doctor Away

No mother wants to see her precious child fall down, bump his noggin, or stub his toe. Unfortunately, these accidents do happen from time to time. When my children hurt, they run to me for support. Most importantly, they want a kiss. Somehow, a kiss from Mommy makes everything better. The tears disappear and a smile returns.

My boys come to me all the time with their hand, leg, or toe stretched out to me. Sometimes I hear, "Mommy hurt" or "Mommy kiss." I know what I am supposed to do. I reach down and I kiss their hurt. Magically, in a matter of minutes and sometimes seconds, they resume playing as if nothing ever happened. They needed my love and my care, and they received it.

As you know, regardless if you are a new mom or an experienced mom, you will encounter bumps and bruises along your life's journey. You will fall down, get discouraged, and cry for help. The good news is, like our children, we too have someone who loves us and cares for us more than anyone else in this world—our heavenly Father. No matter how deep or how wide the pain is you are suffering, God is waiting for you with outstretched arms. As powerful as a mother's kiss is, his is much more powerful and perfect. He is the Great Physician.

If you find yourself struggling with any type of pain—physical, emotional, or spiritual—run like a child toward Jesus. Reach out your hands, your arms, or your whole self to him and shout, "Father hurt. Father kiss." God will help you and comfort you. He is always there for you. Our heavenly Father wants to wipe away your tears and help you smile again.

> Come to Me, all who are weary and heavy-laden, and I will give you rest.
>
> Matthew 11:28 (NASB)

### Take Just a Minute

# You Can Do It

I will never forget when Caleb learned how to put his shoes and socks on all by himself. After he put them on, he looked up at me with his big brown eyes and with a huge smile on his face shouted, "Did it!" He was so excited. He could not wait to share his accomplishment with me. His joy warmed my heart. He is my precious little boy, and I love seeing him learn new things.

God looks at you with this same excitement and pride when you celebrate accomplishments in your life. When you graduated from high school, he clapped. When you got your first job, he rejoiced. And now, as you learn how to care for your children, God is smiling from heaven and cheering you on. He knows balancing diaper changing, grocery shopping, doctors' appointments, house cleaning, and laundry services are no small feats to conquer. His heart warms as you learn and grow as a mother.

We are not perfect and, like Caleb, who sometimes puts his shoes on the wrong feet, we will make mistakes. But just as a mom is always there to encourage and guide her children, God is always there encouraging and guiding you.

I hope you will take some time today to think about how special you are to our Lord. He is your biggest cheerleader. You are so precious to him. Always remember, he created you, and no matter how tough your job as a mom may be, you can do it! God believes in you! Pray for God to help you believe in yourself.

> For you created my inmost being; you knit me together in my mother's womb. I praise you because I am fearfully and wonderfully made; your works are wonderful, I know that full well.
>
> Psalm 139:13–14 (NIV)

### Take Just a Minute

_____

_____

_____

_____

_____

_____

_____

# The Blessing of Friendship

Whether you are sharing exciting news, needing advice on a tough situation, or just chatting about nothing, our friends are there for us. We love our husbands and we adore our children, but as women, we need other like-minded individuals who can relate to us in a way no one else can. We are fortunate when God blesses us with these special people.

Over the past few years, especially now that I have young children, I have come to realize how special my close friends really are. I need them in my life and I would be very lonely without them. I understand how important it is to make time for them, no matter how busy I get with my day-to-day responsibilities.

Just like I need my earthly friends in my life, I need my eternal and best friend, my Lord and Savior Jesus Christ even more. Unfortunately, I often forget to turn to him when I have exciting news to share or hardships I need help with. I imagine Jesus sitting by the phone or maybe looking at his e-mail account and wondering why I haven't contacted him. Just like my girlfriends, he wants me to reach out to him. He wants to rejoice with me when I have good news, and he wants to cry with me and hold me when I am discouraged and sad.

Jesus, more than anyone, understands everything I am going through, no matter how big or how small.

    I am so thankful God has given me such wonderful friends here on earth. I pray you have been blessed with special people you can turn to in the good and bad times. But I am most thankful we can share the "best friend" anyone can have in this world. I am going to give him a call today. I hope you will too!

> Greater love has no one than this, that he lay down his life for his friends. You are my friends if you do what I command. I no longer call you servants, because a servant does not know his master's business. Instead, I have called you friends, for everything that I learned from my father I have made known to you.
>
> John 15:13–15 (NIV)

## Take Just a Minute

_____

_____

_____

_____

_____

# Been on a Date Lately?

Can you remember the last time you spent quality time with your husband, without your children? I don't mean watching the latest DVR recording, or folding laundry together, or cleaning out the garage on a Saturday. I mean genuine, quality time where the two of you just focus on each other and talk together without being pulled in several different directions.

You grab a cup of coffee with your girlfriends, attend a weekly Bible study, participate in a playgroup, and go to church with your family—all of which are great—but are you spending one-on-one time with the man God gave you to love, honor, and cherish for "as long as you both shall live"?

Moms and dads have hectic schedules. Finding time for just each other is a challenge, but it is a challenge worth overcoming. Our children look to us for guidance and direction. Showing our children that Mom and Dad love each other so much they want to be with just each other from time to time will have a tremendous impact on them. It is important for our children to understand Mommy and Daddy need time together to deepen their relationship and strengthen their marriage. I am so thankful God has blessed me with a husband to share my life with. I never want to take him for granted. Just as I want to get to know my girlfriends better, I must show Richard, and my boys, how much more I want to get to know him. I don't want to miss out on the opportunity to grow closer to him as my husband and my friend.

This week I want to encourage you to make a date with your spouse. Go to a drive-in movie, take a walk in the park, or go share an ice cream cone. What you do doesn't matter, but it does matter that you make time to do something. I hope the next time you are asked, "Have you been on a date lately?" you will be able to answer with joy and excitement, "Yes!" You will be blessed and your husband and your children will be blessed too.

> My beloved is mine, and I am his…
>
> Song of Solomon 2:16 (NASB)

> …This is my beloved and this is my friend…
>
> Song of Solomon 5:16 (NASB)

## Take Just a Minute

# God's Peace Is Waiting for You

My husband and I had the most wonderful vacation in Maui, Hawaii—by far the most beautiful place I have ever visited. As I sat on my balcony each morning, I was in awe of the flowers so brilliant with color and the ocean so beautiful and full of life. I could see mountains and trees and the most amazing sky, especially at night. Being in this special place, I couldn't help but think of God and the detailed steps he took to create this magnificent world we live in. I felt so blessed to be able to experience his creation. As I sat there amongst such beauty, my heart was full of joy and appreciation and peace.

I realize now how little time I take to pause and admire God's beautiful artwork. I don't look up at the stars and watch how they twinkle. I don't sit on the grass and just allow the sun to hit my face and feel its warmth. I forget to notice the beautiful wildflowers on the side of the road just dancing in the wind as I drive by each day.

We all have busy schedules. We have shopping to do and meals to prepare. We have carpool duty and soccer practice. We have doctors' appointments and church activities. But is anything more important than appreciating God's creation? How often do I miss the peace God wants me to enjoy because I fail to make time to experience God's beauty—pure and divine?

Take time this week to notice the amazing creation surrounding you. Walk barefoot through a park, feeling the grass between your toes. Watch a sunset, noticing the beautiful colors illuminating the sky. Go for a swim in a lake, feeling the water refresh your whole body. Take time to enjoy all that God has created. Don't wait another minute. God's peace is waiting for you.

> You will go out in joy and be led forth in peace; the mountains and hills will burst into song before you, and all the trees of the field will clap their hands.
>
> Isaiah 55:12 (NIV)

**Take Just a Minute**

_____

_____

_____

_____

_____

# You Know You Are a Mom When...

You know you are a mom when:

- Your alarm is set for twelve a.m., three a.m., six a.m., and nine a.m.
- You cannot remember the last time you took a shower.
- Your shirt, around the shoulder area, has some type of food on it.
- Laundry is an everyday activity, but folding it is not.
- The socks on your feet don't match and your shirt is on inside out.
- You are eating chicken nuggets, macaroni and cheese, or pizza... *again!*
- You tell yourself, "I know I just picked that up."
- The theme songs to *Barney, Clifford,* and the movie *Cars* will not get out of your mind.
- "No" is the most common word used in your home—by both mom and child.

But you also know you are a mom when:

- Three a.m. is one of the most special moments of the day.
- You look into the bedroom when all is quiet and you are certain there is an angel sleeping there.
- Your heart melts when that sweet little voice says, "I love you, Mommy."
- Laughter fills your home.
- Your kiss is the only thing that can make a boo-boo better.
- Hearing your child sing brings you joy and a smile.
- Your fridge is covered with special crafts, photos, and award ribbons.
- You cry on the first day on kindergarten.
- You can't wait for three 'o clock to get here.

Being a mom can be tiring at times, but thankfully, it is worth it. Take a little time to write down your happiest and most exciting motherhood moments. The next time you are feeling weary or discouraged, take it out and read it. Sometimes, all you need to get through the rough times is a reminder of the happy ones.

> For this boy I prayed, and the Lord has given me my petition which I asked of Him. "So I have also dedicated him to the Lord; as long as he lives he is dedicated to the Lord" And he worshiped the Lord there.
>
> 1 Samuel 1:27–28 (NASB)

# Take Just a Minute

# Yes, Mommy Makes Mistakes Too

Moms, lets face it, we make mistakes. Let me share a few:

1. After telling your children to be careful with their drinks and keep them in the kitchen, you spill your drink all over the living room floor.
2. You want your child to get ready for school in a timely manner, but you cannot seem to get them to school on time, even if they dressed themselves just like you asked.
3. You raise your voice when you know you shouldn't.
4. You tell them you will do this or that "later." Later comes, but "this or that" doesn't.
5. You set a limit on how much TV they can watch, but you are tired because you stayed up too late watching your favorite shows.

6. You realize your son or daughter was telling the truth after you disciplined them.

Over the past five years, I have had to humble myself many times before my children. At first, I would wallow in my mistakes (which is what Satan wants us to do.) It is difficult to admit to anyone, especially your children, that Mommy makes mistakes too. Fortunately, I have come to realize, through my mistakes, that I have a great opportunity to teach my children how to admit their mistakes, the importance of repenting from their mistakes, to do their best to correct their mistakes, and to strive not to repeat it. Although I am not proud of my mistakes, I want my children to realize they are not alone in their struggles to do what is right. Mommy understands what they are going through. I want them to come to me and know that I will always love them.

Don't allow Satan to tell you that you are not a good mom or that you don't know what you are doing. Look to God for direction and guidance and forgiveness when you mess up. Ask him to help you turn these situations into "teachable moments" for your children. Just as you love your children when they make mistakes, God loves you as well. He will never leave you. He will always help you. He will always love you.

> Be strong and courageous. Do not be afraid or terrified because of them, for the Lord your God goes with you; he will never leave you nor forsake you.
>
> Deuteronomy 31:6 (NIV)

## Take Just a Minute

# Jesus Took the Nails

My boys and I were working on a craft project, which is rare in our house due to my lack of creativity. I gave the boys markers, stickers, and construction paper, and I asked them to make two name plates. Clay and Caleb, only two and three at the time, worked very hard on this project. After they were done, I was excited to admire their work.

Caleb did a great job of making wild marks on his paper. He also applied as many stickers as he could fit onto his creation. I loved it. Clay had used stickers as well, but I was in awe of what he had created. I wish you could see it and hear him explain it. He showed me how he had positioned the stickers to make a cross and how at the bottom was Jesus's bloodstained feet. He even told me one of the stickers represented the nails Jesus endured. I could not believe how serious he was as he described in his special way our Lord's crucifixion.

After showing me his creation, Clay picked up his children's Bible and brought it over to me. He wanted to find the picture of Jesus on the cross. I helped him locate it, and then we talked together about Jesus and how he died on the cross for our sins. I was overjoyed that a simple art project turned into such a special time.

Later that day, we were driving down the road and Clay misbehaved in the back seat. I told him what he had done was a sin. He then proceeded to say, "Will I get nails in my feet too?" I was able to tell him, as we had discussed earlier that morning, "No, Jesus took the nails for us." Isn't it wonderful when we can talk to our children about what Jesus did for us and for them? Clay doesn't understand the gospel completely yet, but I see him starting to realize how special a relationship with Jesus is. This delights me beyond words. It is my deepest prayer to see Clay and Caleb make a decision to believe and put their trust in our Lord. I know it is your dream for your child too.

I really want to encourage you to listen to your children. Be aware of what they are leaning about our Lord. Be prepared to answer their questions and take time to ask them questions as well. Seek God's direction. Pray with your kids, read Bible stories, and memorize Scripture together. Never miss an opportunity to teach your children about the love of Christ. They really do understand more than you probably know. What a blessing we have as parents to be able to teach our children about God, and what an even bigger blessing to see our children receive his love.

> So commit yourselves wholeheartedly to these words of mine...Teach them to your children. Talk about them when you are at home and when you are on the road, when you are going to bed and when you are getting up.
>
> Deuteronomy 11:18–19 (NLT)

# Take Just a Minute

# Creativity Equals Chaos

I went into my boys' playroom to find their three-tiered bookshelf dismantled. Everything it once held was scattered about the floor. I wanted to scream, "What in the world is going on here?" It took a great deal of self-control not to. I paused for a moment and asked the boys, semi-calmly, why they had taken the bookshelf apart. As they gave their explanation, I couldn't help but smile. "We are giving each other haircuts."

You see, they had been to the barber shop with their dad, and they wanted to reenact their outing. They were using the three bookshelf parts as chairs and their toolset as hair cutting supplies. Pretty creative, I had to admit. Now that I was in their room, they wanted to include me in their fun. Clay lined up the three shelves, one for me, one for Caleb, and one for him. I then had the privilege of having my hair cut and then cutting the boy's hair. It was a special time.

If your home is like mine, it usually feels more like a child's playground than a sanctuary. Rather than a place of refuge and relaxation, it is often a place of disorder and distress. Moms, I want to encourage you. You can experience joy and excitement in the middle of such disarray.

Try this. The next time you see a mud pie on your doorstep, don't think "Oh no, my son's hands are going to be so dirty." Go outside, grab a handful of mud, and ask your little one to show you how to make a pie just like theirs. If there is magic marker on your walls, don't think about how long it is going to take to clean it, be glad you purchased washable markers. Who knows, your child may be an artist someday and you can say, "I knew you when..." If you try, I know you can change the way you view your child's messes. Don't always put an immediate stop to their fun. Join them. Get dirt on your face or paint on your arms. Allow yourself to be creative. The memories you make will last a lot longer than the time it takes you to clean up afterward.

Our Lord does not want messes, ours or our children's, to cause us despair. He wants us to be joyful. Spend time in prayer today. Allow God to give you a spirit of gladness and not one of mourning. Ask him to help you see the beauty among the ashes your children create. Give thanks for their creativity. If you will seek our faithful Lord, I know he will help you find the peace you need to survive the chaos. And, who knows? You may even have a little fun in the process.

> The Spirit of the Sovereign Lord is on me, because the Lord has anointed me to preach good news to the poor... to proclaim the year of the Lord's favor... and provide for those who grieve in Zion—to bestow on them a crown of beauty instead of ashes, the oil of gladness instead of mourning, and a garment of praise instead of a spirit of despair...
>
> Isaiah 61:1–3 (NIV)

# Take Just a Minute

# You Can Admit It. You Are Tired.

- It's three a.m. Your baby is hungry. You are tired.
- It's eight a.m. Your child has been up sick all night. You are tired.
- It's eleven a.m. You have taken one child to preschool, another to a doctor's appointment, and you need to finish the meal you are taking over to a friend. You are tired.
- Not sure what time it is now, but your baby is ready to eat again. Tired.
- It's four p.m. Time to straighten the house and prepare dinner. Still tired.
- It's five p.m. Time to feed your baby again. So tired.
- It's seven p.m. Time to get the kids bathed and ready for bed. You are really tired.
- It's midnight. Your baby is hungry. You are beyond tired.

We try so hard to be superwoman, but too often we end up feeling like a withered flower. We tell our friends or our husband everything is okay, even though we can hardly think straight. We feel like something must be wrong with us because we cannot do it all. Let me encourage you today: nothing is wrong with you. You are perfectly normal. But you do need to reach out to others and admit you need some help. Here are a few suggestions to help you get through those tiresome days:

- Ask your husband to take a feeding shift or bring in a pizza for dinner. Sometimes, husbands don't realize we need help. They too think we can "do it all" and need a little friendly reminder that, sometimes, we can't.

- Allow one of your close friends to come over and watch the kids so you can take a nap, especially if you have a newborn. Remember, they have been there and would love to help. It would bless them more than you know.

- Realize you do not have to have a perfect house, especially when you have a newborn. It is okay if the toys are not always picked up, the beds are unmade, or the dishes are still in the sink. An imperfect house does not make you a poor mom. Energy for your children and your husband is much more important. Trust me, your family will thank you for it.

- The most important suggestion I would like to give you is to reach out to the Lord when you need an extra burst of energy. He will get you through those tough times when you don't think you can go on. He knows better than anyone how you are feeling.

I am so thankful for my friends and family who have helped me along the way, especially during my early days of motherhood. I appreciate them more than they will ever know. Dear sweet Mom, these tiresome days will not last forever. The stresses of having young children are only temporary. Praise the Lord! Tell the Lord today if you are struggling. Seek his strength and support. He desires to help you in your time of need. Don't get discouraged. Brighter days are ahead. You can do this.

> God is our refuge and strength, an ever-present help in trouble.
>
> Psalm 46:1 (NIV)

### Take Just a Minute

_____

_____

_____

_____

_____

_____

_____

_____

# Do I Really Have to Leave the Hospital?

Being a new mom is one of the most exciting, rewarding, and challenging experiences of a woman's life. The first time you hold that precious baby in your arms, you are filled with a love only a mother can understand. The sound of their first cry, the feel of their new baby skin, the amazement over how tiny their little fingers and toes are is indescribable. On the day your little boy or little girl is born, you know without a doubt miracles really do happen. Praise the Lord!

No matter how wonderful the first couple of days can be, if you are like most moms—or at least if you are like me—the joy can turn to fear when it's time to leave the hospital or say goodbye to your extended family as they head back to their own home. It is now time for you, with the help of your husband, to take care of this little bundle of joy all by yourself. Yikes!

Let me encourage you. If you feel scared or uncertain about your new responsibility, you are perfectly normal, and you can do this. You really can. During those first few days and weeks as you experience mixed emotions of fear and joy; remember, God entrusted women with the important task of childbearing and motherhood. He entrusted you. What an awesome feeling. God chose you, only you, to bear and raise your little angel. What an honor and blessing you have been bestowed.

Spend time with the Lord today. Praise him for the gift of motherhood. Praise him for your children. Take any fears or doubts about your mothering abilities directly to God. Ask him to give you courage and confidence. God has faith in you. Believe in yourself. Remember, you are not alone in this journey. God is always with you.

> Now the man called his wife's name Eve, because she was the mother of all the living.
>
> Genesis 3:20 (NASB)

> Jesus looked at them and said, "With man this is impossible, but with God all things are possible."
>
> Matthew 19:26 (NIV)

# Take Just a Minute

# Searching for God

In the mornings when my son Caleb wakes up, I can hear the pitter-patter of his little feet as he runs through the house looking for his momma. Sometimes I will just lie in my bed, awaiting his precious arrival. I love his beautiful smile when he finds me. He is truly happy to be in my presence, and I cannot wait to wrap my arms around him and hold him close. Caleb makes me feel so wanted and needed, and I want nothing more than to give him those same feelings in return.

Isn't this a great representation of our God? I believe he wants us to search for him each day with the same fervor Caleb exhibits when he searches for me. God desires and deserves to be sought after. He wants to bring a huge smile and joy to our lives. Just as I wait with anticipation to see Caleb at my bedside, I believe God looks down from heaven and waits for us each morning to run to him. God cannot wait to hold us close.

Are you searching for God every day? Does he know you desire to be in his presence? Can you feel his warmth, his love, his desire to be with you? Are you spending time with him each day? Does he know how much you love him? Do you make God feel wanted and needed? I know life gets busy, but it should never be too busy for God. Remember, he watches over you and listens for you every day and every night. He loves you so much.

I want to encourage you to seek after God with all your heart. Run to him as a child runs to his mother. Think about the happiness you feel when you see your child running towards you and smiling at you. Go now! Don't wait! God will be waiting for you with open arms.

> "But from there you will seek the Lord your God, and you will find Him if you search for Him with all your heart and all your soul."
>
> Deuteronomy 4:29 (NASB)

## Take Just a Minute

_____

_____

_____

_____

_____

_____

# Because It Makes You Happy

I was sitting outside in the boys' playhouse. Clay and Caleb were in the sandbox below, working diligently. Clay soon appeared by my side with a big, yellow bucket. Very excitedly, he told me this was a present for me! With much appreciation, and a little bit of curiosity, I took the bucket from him and looked inside. The bucket was filled with Legos and sand. I wish you could have seen the smile and excitement on his face as I "opened" the gift. It might have only been sand and toys, but no gift could have meant more to me at that moment.

I wasn't sure why I had been honored with such a unique gift. It wasn't my birthday. It wasn't Mother's Day. I hadn't asked Clay to make me anything. When I asked Clay why he gave me this special gift, he replied without hesitation, "Because it makes you happy!" My heart began to melt.

I was amazed that, at the tender age of three and a half, my son wanted to do something not because he wanted anything in return, but because he simply wanted to make me happy. Wow! Clay had no idea how special or how loved it would make me feel. He represented exactly how God wants all of us to live out our lives—showing selfless love and kindness. Clay could not have made me feel more loved that day. I was so proud of him.

Take time to praise your children when they do special things for others. I also want to encourage you to do something soon for someone else. As Clay reminded me, it doesn't have to be fancy or expensive, just something from your heart that shows you care. Just as Clay's face lit up when he gave me his sand-filled present, I wish you that same joy as you do something just "because it makes them happy." What a wonderful way to honor our Lord.

> "In everything I showed you that by working hard in this manner you must help the weak and remember the words of the Lord Jesus, that He Himself said, 'It is more blessed to give than to receive.'"
>
> Acts 20:35 (NASB)

### Take Just a Minute

_____

_____

_____

_____

# So Proud of Me?

As we were driving down the road one day, Clay shouted excitedly, "Caleb didn't take his seatbelt off!" You have no idea how relieved I was to hear this. You see, Caleb had just moved into a big-boy car seat and, unfortunately, learned all too quickly how to unhook his seatbelt. I would look in my rearview mirror while in motion and see Caleb standing in the backseat or turned around looking out the back window—not safe for anyone, especially a two-year-old. I had been trying very hard to teach him the importance of keeping his seatbelt on. I desperately wanted Caleb to obey for his safety and for my sanity.

It thrilled me so much that Caleb obeyed my instructions, but it equally thrilled me that Clay, his big brother, made such a big deal out of Caleb's obedience. It prompted me to quickly tell Caleb how proud I was he kept his seatbelt on. This was such an important moment. In the absolute sweetest voice Caleb replied, "So proud of me?" I wish you could have heard the tenderness he expressed. I could tell my words of praise really meant a lot to him. Even at two years old, Caleb wanted to know his mommy was proud of him. Like all of us, Caleb needed more than instructions on what to do or not do; he needed praise and affirmation. We expect a lot from our little ones, don't we? Don't touch this, or stay away from that. Say please and thank you. Don't climb on the table. Stay in your seat. Don't hit your brother. Sometimes, we find ourselves focusing on what our children are not doing correctly rather than acknowledging what they are doing right. I know I have certainly been guilty. Just as the master showed his praise to the slaves who multiplied their talents, and just as God showed his love for his Son when he was transfigured on the mountain, it is so important as a mom to make special efforts to praise our children. We must not let the tiniest steps they are taking in the right direction go unnoticed, especially when it comes to obedience. I love the joy I see on my boys' faces when they hear me acknowledge their efforts.

Take time today to reflect on an area in your child's life where you have seen progress. Maybe they cleared their dishes off the table without being asked, brushed their teeth without complaining, or shared their favorite toy. I know you can think of something if you really try. Just as our Lord shows us repeatedly how proud he is of us through his blessings and answered prayers, say or do something special today to let them know you are so proud of them. I guarantee it will make a difference in your child's life and in your life as well.

> For he received honor and glory from God the father when the voice came to him from the Majestic Glory, saying, "This is my Son, whom I love; with him I am well pleased." We ourselves heard this voice that came from heaven when we were with him on the sacred mountain.
>
> 2 Peter 1:17–18 (NIV)

## Take Just a Minute

# Have You Seen My Hurt, Dada?

My boys love to show off their "hurts." Whether it is to the cashier at Walmart, their friends at playgroup, or their grandparents, they love to point out the scrape on their leg or the scratch on their face.

My boys will go back and forth with my husband, Richard, saying, "Have you seen *my* hurt, Dada?" says Clay.

"Have you seen *my* hurt?" follows Caleb. It is not uncommon for my boys to talk days, weeks, and sometimes months later about a hurt I can no longer see. I am amazed they can hang on to their injuries for such a long time.

I am a lot like my children in this area. How many hurts do I hold onto long after an incident occurred? Don't I still bring up past hurt feelings with my husband? Don't I still feel embarrassed about the times my children acted up at Chick-Fil-A? What about my dear friend or family member who betrayed me? Am I not still upset and angry? Unfortunately, the answer to most of these questions is yes. Can you relate? Are their "hurts" in your life you still talk or think about? What pain are you holding on to?

We, as moms, have the wonderful blessing of providing comfort, hugs, and Spiderman band-aids when our children have a hurt. Hopefully, we also take time to help them let go of the pain and move past the difficult experience. We do not want them to remain in suffering, whether physical or mental. We want our children to enjoy life and live it to the fullest.

God wants this for you too. He gives us comfort, support, and love, and through his Word teaches us how to move past our pain on to true healing. He does not want you to be held captive to past pain. I am reminded there is nothing God cannot conquer.

Spend time in prayer today. Take any hurts you have been holding on to straight to our Lord and Savior. I pray as you seek his help that you will experience joy, peace, and healing like you have never known before.

> I have told you these things, so that in me you may have peace. In this world you will have trouble. But take heart! I have overcome the world.
>
> John 16:33 (NIV)

> Do not let your hearts be troubled. Trust in God; trust also in me.
>
> John 14:1 (NIV)

# Take Just a Minute

# Someday, When I Get Bigger

Someday, when I get bigger:

- I am going to tie my shoes all by myself.
- I am going to jump off buildings like Spiderman. Yikes!
- I am going to wear my dad's shoes.
- I am going to drive Dad's truck and Caleb is going to sit up front with me. Mom and Dad can sit in the back.
- I am going to have a blue bicycle.
- My hair is going to fall out too (like my dad's.) Then we will both have no hair.
- I am going to work with my friend Jaden.
- I am going to buy a blue airplane and Momma can get a pink one.

Clay gets so excited when he tells me his plans for the future. He is filled with confidence and joy. Both my boys fully embrace life. They do not live in fear or trouble themselves with worry. They are happy and carefree. They believe in the hope and joy awaiting them.

Isn't this exactly what God desires for all his children, and for you? He wants us—children and parents—to embrace life, without fear, trusting in him every step of the way. He wants us to experience life with hope, joy, and excitement. God does not want his children to worry or dread what lies ahead. He wants us to understand he is in control and he has great plans for each of us.

Take a moment today to think about the little things your children look forward to. What are some of the things you looked forward to when you were younger? What are the things you look forward to now? What is keeping you from making your dreams come true? Spend time in prayer today. Hand over your concerns and anxieties to our Lord. He wants you to have confidence and hope in your future. God wants you to experience life with the same joy and excitement as your child. God has a perfect plan just for you.

> "For I know the plans I have for you," declares the Lord, "plans to prosper you and not to harm you, plans to give you hope and a future."
>
> Jeremiah 29:11 (NIV)

## Take Just a Minute

# I Know Where You Are

Caleb loves to come into our room in the middle of the night. Sometimes he feels sick. Sometimes he is scared. Sometimes he is lonely and needs someone (usually me) to hold him. When he was younger, he would yell for me to come and get him, but now, no matter the time or how dark it is, he makes his way to my room on his own. Caleb has made the familiar trip so many times that he doesn't even need to turn on a light to direct his path. He knows exactly where he needs to go for comfort, protection, and love—and he knows exactly how to get there. He has complete trust and faith that when he arrives, he will be accepted. and, of course, he is.

Isn't this a wonderful example of how God wants us to seek him? Just as Caleb trusts in me, God wants his children to trust and have faith in him. He wants us to run without hesitation to *his* side when we need guidance, love, and support. God wants us to know that he will always accept us.

Do you know where to find God? Do you fully trust in him and his promises? Do you turn to him for peace, or do you stay where you are alone and afraid? Are you spending time in prayer and do you read his precious Word? Can you run safely into his arms with the lights off, or do you get lost along the way? How well do you really know God?

God loves you and knows you better than anyone else in this world. Let me encourage you to take time today to really seek him and know him more. I hope you will reach out to our precious Lord more often and more passionately than ever before.

> I am the good shepherd, and I know My own and My own know Me.
>
> John 10:14 (NASB)

## Take Just a Minute

_____

_____

_____

_____

_____

_____

# Following the Leader

I am amazed by the influence Clay has on his little brother, Caleb. I have never seen anything like it. "Where's Clay?" or "want Clay," are popular phrases. If Clay wears blue jeans, Caleb wants to wear blue jeans. If Clay runs and then falls down, Caleb will run to the exact spot and fall down. One day, Clay accidentally dropped the ball he was playing with, so Caleb found a ball and dropped it. Caleb even knocked his cup over on purpose one day because Clay spilled his milk on accident. At the tender age of five, Clay is already a leader and an example for Caleb—good or bad.

As I think about the role model Clay is for his little brother, I am reminded of the special individuals who have impacted me in amazing ways. At the top of the list is my family: my parents, my grandparents, and, of course, my husband. I am so thankful for the positive examples they set for me. I can only hope and pray Clay and Caleb will be a positive influence on each other and on the people close to them.

Just like Caleb looks up to his big brother and I look up to my family, God desires for his children to look up to him. God loves us so much. He provides so many wonderful examples for us to follow in his precious Word. In an effort to protect us and guide us, he never stops being the leader we should all strive to follow. We are so blessed.

I hope you will take a moment to reflect on the people who have impacted your life—past and present. Have you told them how much they mean to you and how thankful you are for them? How has God impacted your life? Have you praised him for all he has taught you and continues to teach you? Is God your top priority, and are you striving to follow his example?

Tell God how much you love him today. Thank him for being such a great role model. If you haven't been following God like you need to, confess that to him and start now. Just as Caleb walks around the house saying "I want Clay Binns." I hope you will spend time today saying, "I want Jesus." Let him be your leader today and for the rest of your life. God will not lead you astray.

> My sheep hear My voice, and I know them, and they follow Me.
>
> John 10:27 (NASB)

> But Ruth said, "Do not urge me to leave you or turn back from following you; for where you go, I will go, and where you lodge, I will lodge. Your people shall be my people, and your God, my God."
>
> Ruth 1:16 (NASB)

## Take Just a Minute

# Can We Have a Mommy Day Today?

One morning, Clay asked me the sweetest question. He said, "Can we have a mommy day today?" He explained this was a day where we didn't have to go anywhere—not to pre-school, not to mommy's Bible study, not to Walmart, not anywhere. This was a day where we just stayed at home and spent time together. I was touched and thrilled by his request and, of course, I said, "Yes!"

Until Clay asked for this special day, I didn't realize how busy the boys and I were. Although I am a stay-at-home mom, we are out and about a lot. We usually do productive activities like grocery shopping, playgroups, or church activities, but all of those activities occur outside our home. On this day, Clay reminded me how important it is to just play and have fun at home. We didn't need to spend so much time running from one activity to the next. I was amazed what I learned from my little boy. Children teach us so much.

It is important to notice the value Christ placed on little children. Christ knew they needed attention from him. He loved children with all his heart and did not fail to make time for them, no matter how busy he was. As a mom, we must follow his example. Our children need attention from us too—unhindered attention.

Moms, I want to encourage you to take time out of your busy schedule just to hang out with your little ones. Make pancakes in fun shapes or letters (a favorite at our house.) Build a castle out of blocks. Make a paper airplane and fly it around the house. Get a little messy and finger paint. Shoot hoops or throw a football. Ask your children what they want to do. I know you will make memories your children will never forget.

Tell God today how much you love your children and how thankful you are for them. Ask God to help you organize your schedule so that you really do "stay-at-home." If you work outside the home, ask God to help you find creative ways to spend time with them—on your lunch break, before school, before they go to bed. Allow God to help you grow closer to your children as you spend quality time with them every day. I pray your "Mommy Days" will mean as much to you and your children as they mean to me.

> Then little children were brought to Jesus for him to place his hands on them and pray for them. But the disciples rebuked those who brought them. Jesus said, "Let the little children come to me, and do not hinder them, for the kingdom of heaven belongs to such as these."
>
> Matthew 19:13–14 (NIV)

# Take Just a Minute

# Momma, I Love You

Caleb woke me up one morning in the most wonderful way. He touched me softly and said in the sweetest voice, "Momma, I love you." It was first thing in the morning, so I hadn't done anything to earn his affection. I hadn't made him breakfast or read him a story. I hadn't bought him anything. As I looked down at his precious face, I realized he didn't even want anything in return. What an amazing feeling. I sat there smiling, knowing without a doubt I was special to him.

Isn't this a wonderful example of how we should demonstrate love for our heavenly Father? How delighted would God be to hear, "I love you, Lord," each morning before we ask anything of him? Wouldn't it please God to hear how much we appreciate him before he answers our prayers or a blessing is given? Can you imagine the joy on his magnificent face when we exhibit love in such an unconditional way? We can learn a lot from our children.

I encourage you to take a few moments today to tell your little ones thank you for all they teach *you*. They are such blessings. Most importantly, I hope you will take time each day to tell our Lord and Savior how much you love him, not because of what he has done for you, but for who *he* is. No one deserves it more.

> Jesus replied: "Love the Lord your God with all your heart and with all your soul and with all your mind." This is the first and greatest commandment.
>
> Matthew 22:37–38 (NIV)

## Take Just a Minute

_____

_____

_____

_____

_____

_____

_____

_____

# I Love Room Check

When I first brought my boys home from the hospital, I constantly checked on them during the night. Were they breathing okay? Did they have a fever? Were they crying? I couldn't bear the thought of anything happening to them. I always wanted to be there if they needed me. I even slept on the floor by Clay's crib during those first precious days of his life because I wanted to be close to him and listen to his little baby noises.

As Clay and Caleb grow older, I find myself continuing to check on them several times each night. I still want to make sure they are sleeping okay. If they have been sick, I want to make sure their condition hasn't worsened. Sometimes, I just want to make sure they are not too hot or too cold. Some nights I crawl up next to Clay and Caleb and whisper into their little ears how much I love them and how special they are to me.

The most special part of my late-night room checks is the time I spend in prayer in the room they share. As I look at their peaceful bodies curled up into precious sleeping positions, I get down on my knees between their two beds and I praise God for the gift he has given me. I pray for their salvation, for their protection, for their future spouse, and for their purity. Just like when they were babies, I can't bear the thought of anything happening to them, and I want to take every opportunity to pray for them and lift them up to the Lord. I cherish this special nighttime activity.

As I think about my nighttime routine, I am reminded of how our heavenly Father is always checking in on us. It is amazing to think about how God loves each of us with an even deeper love than the love we have for our children. Wow! Our Father is always looking in on us to make sure we are doing okay. He wants to protect us, guide us, heal us, and just be there for us, no matter what we are going through. What a blessing we have in him.

The next time you look in on your little ones, take a moment to think about how our Lord checks in on you. He loves you so much. He will always be there for you, watching over you and offering you comfort and protection. Never forget how special you are to our Lord!

> As a mother comforts her child, so will I comfort you; and you will be comforted over Jerusalem.
>
> Isaiah 66:13 (NIV)

> Now I am departing from the world; they are staying in this world, but I am coming to you. Holy father, you have given me your name; now protect them by the power of your name so that they will be united just as we are.
>
> John 17:11 (NLT)

## Take Just a Minute

# Where's the Pink?

When I was a little girl, I loved to play with Barbie dolls, Strawberry Shortcake, and Care Bears. Almost every Sunday, I would go over to my grandmother Don's house and spend hours playing dress-up, wearing her high-heeled shoes and twirling around in her old formals. My little pink desk was one of my favorite places to be. I could not describe a track hoe or a front-end loader. Bugs were "so gross," and I was not a big fan of the outdoors.

My, how things change when you are the mommy of two little boys. The only doll in our home is mine from when I was a little girl. Clay and Caleb turn toast, cheese, tools, and train tracks into some type of shooting device. There is a ball in every room, and "Mom, can I go outside?" is one of the most commonly asked questions. Oh, did I mention worms and bugs are "so cool"? No pink My Little Ponies or tea parties here.

I was so excited when I found out we were having a little boy, but I was a little anxious about raising someone so different than myself. Could I be the mom Clay and Caleb needed? Would I be "fun" enough or "exciting" enough? Would they want to spend time with their mommy, or would they count the hours until dad got home? I knew there would be challenges to overcome. What I didn't know was that having these two energetic, rambunctious little boys would be the greatest gift I could have ever been given.

Until Clay and Caleb, I never thought I would enjoy throwing a ball or building a tower just to knock it down again. I never thought being locked up in "pretend" jail or having my hair cut with a toy saw would be so much fun. My boys bring me more laughter than I could ever have imagined, and I am so thankful God has given me such a wonderful opportunity to be their mom.

Moms, I want to encourage you today. Your children may be completely different from you. You may have a little girl who loves frilly dresses when you prefer jeans and a T-shirt. You may not have a musical bone in your body, but your son wants to try every musical instrument he can get his hands on. You might have a huge fear of spiders, but your little angel wants very badly to have a bug collection—in your home! Even if you feel totally unprepared to be the mom your child needs, don't be afraid. God is prepared.

Take any cares and concerns you have about raising your children straight to the Lord today. Ask him to guide you when you feel lost or insecure. God knew who your children were going to be before they were born, and he knew you would be their mom. He knows your child's favorite toy, color, and activity, and he knows you can adapt to their interests if they are different from yours. You might be amazed at how much joy their differences bring you. I pray as you embrace the interest of your children, your children will embrace you.

No pink here? I don't care. I say, "Bring on the blue!"

> Trust in the Lord with all your heart, and lean not on your own understanding; in all your ways acknowledge Him, and He shall direct your paths.
>
> Proverbs 3:5–6 (NKJV)

## Take Just a Minute

# Momma, Momma—Airplane!

I love how excited my boys get over the littlest things. We will be driving down the road and Caleb will shout joyfully, "Tractor moving!" I can bring home raisin bread from the grocery store and they cheer. My boys get the biggest smiles on their faces when they blow bubbles, go down a bumpy dirt road, or see dump trucks unloading dirt on the ground.

When Clay was two, we were playing outside. All of the sudden he yelled, very excitedly, "Momma, Momma—airplane!" Richard and I looked at him and were amazed at the joy he expressed over a plane he saw up in the sky. He was pointing and smiling as if he had seen the greatest thing in the world. And, to Clay, it probably felt that way. I love how my boys delight in today rather than worry about tomorrow. I wish I could be more like them.

Watching my boys embrace life reminds me how God's Word teaches us not to worry. God has promised us he will take care of all of our needs. He does not want us to get caught up in the day-to-day worries life has to offer. He wants us to enjoy life just like our children do. When was the last time you really did just that?

I want to encourage you to spend a little time today thinking about the simple things that bring you joy. Maybe it is the smell of homemade bread. Maybe it is the beauty of fresh flowers growing in your garden. Maybe it is just the joy you feel when your husband gets home from work or when your children get home from school. Thank God today for taking care of you and your family and for the little blessings life has brought your way.

> So do not worry about tomorrow; for tomorrow will care for itself. Each day has enough trouble of its own.
>
> Matthew 6:34 (NASB)

## Take Just a Minute

_____

_____

_____

_____

_____

# Full Speed Ahead

Richard and I always know when Caleb is about to enter a room. We can hear the rapid movements of his little feet as he travels across the floor. It doesn't matter if he is on his way to greet us in the morning, coming to the breakfast table, or helping fetch a ball for his brother Clay, he always travels at the same quick speed. Caleb races after life with enthusiasm and joy. He believes nothing will stand in his way. He truly lives life to the fullest.

God desires all of his children to live an abundant life. Unfortunately, if you are like me, you get too caught up in your normal day-to-day "mommy duties" to think about the additional plans God has for you. You don't really race after life. You move about on auto pilot. You are happy and content, but there is something inside of you saying, "Am I doing everything God is calling me to do?" It doesn't matter if you are a homemaker or if you work outside the home, God may have a special project or opportunity waiting for you, but you haven't allowed yourself to see it.

Take a moment and ask yourself the following questions. What, apart from your family, brings you joy and happiness? What do you get excited about? What do you dream about? Maybe you have dreamt of writing a novel or painting a picture or continuing your education. Maybe you wanted to learn how to sew or play the piano. Have you taken the time to go after your dreams? What is holding you back? Is it guilt? Is it fear? It is uncertainty?

We are so blessed God desires an abundant life for his children. God wants to help us realize our dreams. As long as you keep God first and your family second, you should feel secure about reaching toward what God has prepared for you to accomplish.

Spend time with the Lord today. Take your dreams and desires straight to him. Ask God to show you his will. Ask him to remove any obstacles standing in the way. It is time to turn off the cruise control button. Travel like my little boy Caleb—full speed ahead—into the wonderful plans God has for you.

What are you waiting for?

> I am the door; if anyone enters through Me, he will be saved, and will go in and out and find pasture. The thief comes only to steal and kill and destroy; I came that they may have life, and have it abundantly. I am the good shepherd; the good shepherd lays down His life for the sheep.
>
> John 10:9–11 (NASB)

> I have told you these things so that you will be filled with my joy. Yes, your joy will overflow!
>
> John 15:11 (NLT)

# Take Just a Minute

# Waiting at the Window

When Richard leaves for work in the morning, Clay and Caleb immediately stop what they are doing, run to his side, and give him a hug. Then they run to the front window, press their little hands against the glass, and wait for Richard to pull his truck out of the driveway. When Richard reaches the portion of the road directly in front of their window, he pauses just long enough to wave to the boys. Very excitedly, the boys wave back, shouting, "Bye bye, Dada. We love you."

Unfortunately, there are days when Richard forgets to stop. I see the sadness on the boys' faces as they watch their daddy drive by. "Dada didn't stop!" they cry. I will immediately call Richard on his cell phone and, if I can reach him, he will turn around and come back. After stopping for a quick moment, he once again heads off to work and the boys are happy and ready to resume their day. My boys need that special window time with their dad. They need to witness his love.

There are also times when, for one reason or another, Richard comes to a stop in front on the window, and the boys are not there. No smiling little faces. No tiny hands waving, no voices saying, "I love you, Dad" or

"Have a good day." Richard loves Clay and Caleb so much. He treasures the precious moments he shares with them—no matter how big or how small. When they are not there, his day is less complete. He misses the joy their window time brings.

Watching this interaction between my boys and Richard exemplifies our interaction with our heavenly Father. God has given us the most wonderful gift—the gift of prayer. Just as the boys wait at the window for Richard to stop on the road, God waits patiently, hoping we will come to him. He wants to wave at us each morning and tell us how much he loves us. He wants to guide us and encourage us and help us meet our needs. Unlike Richard, who may sometimes forget to stop, God will never forget. God's window is always open.

Do you run to God every morning, open the window, and pour out your heart to him? Do you tell him each day how much you love him? Do you listen and give him an opportunity to share his love for you? Or, do you leave our Lord paused on the side of the road, watching and wishing you were there? Take time to be with God every day. Don't leave him waiting for you. Don't miss out on the joy, peace, and comfort he wants to give you. And don't miss out on the joy you can give him. His hands are waving. Are you ready to wave back?

> Behold, I stand at the door and knock; if anyone hears my voice and opens the door, I will come in to him and will dine with him, and he with me.
>
> Revelation 3:20 (NASB)

# Take Just a Minute

# Don't Miss Out

How many times have you asked your children to try something new only to hear, "I don't like it," "I'm scared," or "maybe later"? You serve an unfamiliar vegetable or a new casserole and they push it aside before taking one bite. You buy them a new pair of shoes, but they prefer to wear their old shoes—even though they are falling apart. You encourage them to participate in a church or school activity, but they beg you not to make them go. They are unable to grasp how great an opportunity or how good for them these new experiences might be. Often, our children choose to miss out on a potentially great opportunity.

Isn't this exactly how we treat our heavenly Father? Maybe you have been asked to teach a Sunday school class, but you declined. You are happy and comfortable where you are. An opportunity to facilitate a women's small group opened up, but you don't think you are knowledgeable enough. You feel called to serve on the hospitality committee at your church, but you just don't think you have the time. It is amazing how much we have in common with our children. We say no to something before we even give it a chance.

Do you have a fear of the unknown? Have you been listening to your own desires rather than the desires of our Lord? When we fail to pursue his requests, we are missing out on more than a fun experience or a healthy meal; we are missing out on an amazing opportunity to serve our precious Lord. What opportunities have you turned down recently?

As a mom, I know our schedules are full. We cannot say yes to everything asked of us. However, it is important to reach out to the Lord before we say no to an opportunity to serve him. Spend time with the Lord today. Ask him where he is calling you. If you are afraid, ask him for confidence. If you lack knowledge, ask him to teach you. If you think you are too busy, ask him to help you adjust your schedule. If you choose to follow his desires, he will give you the support and direction you need.

Just as we want the best for our children, God wants the best for you. Listen to him today. Follow where he is leading you. Trust in him to guide you. Don't miss out on the wonderful blessings he has planned for you as you serve him and his kingdom.

> Who is the man who fears the Lord? He will instruct him in the way he should choose.
>
> Psalm 25:12 (NASB)

> The Lord says, "I will guide you along the best pathway for your life. I will advise you and watch over you."
>
> Psalm 32:8 (NLT)

## Take Just a Minute

# Celebrate the "Ahhh" Moments

As a mom of a two young children, my house can be pretty chaotic. Our kitchen floor serves as a trash can. Clay and Caleb play with every toy they own—at the same time. They view our living room furniture as an indoor playground. Wrestling is not just on TV. "Please pick up," "please stop," and "please don't hit your brother" can be heard throughout the house several times a day. Sometimes I just want to run to my room, shut the door, and scream. Have you ever felt that way?

Thankfully, there are also times in our home when the boys will say or do something unexpected. Caleb woke up from his nap one day, went into his playroom and just started cleaning up without being asked. After Caleb broke a candleholder Clay cleaned up the mess before I ever saw it. Clay and I were walking through the house, and out of the blue, Clay said, "Mom, I love you!" These are the actions that cause the little things driving me crazy to fade far away into the background. I call these special moments my "Ahhh" moments. These are the moments that help me realize that my children really do listen to me. They are learning. They do care about others. These moments bring me so much joy.

I want to encourage you to take time today to focus on the "Ahhh" moments you experience with your children. Make a list of those moments in a notebook or journal. Take out your list the next time you need a stress reliever. Thank God today for all your children are learning and for the blessings they bring you during the peace and the chaos.

> Rejoice evermore. Pray without ceasing. In every thing give thanks: for this is the will of God in Christ Jesus concerning you.
>
> 1 Thessalonians 5:16–18 (KJV)

**Take Just a Minute**

_____

_____

_____

_____

_____

_____

_____

# No Matter What

Until Clay and Caleb were born, I never really grasped the true meaning of unconditional love. From the moment I found out I was expecting, they had my heart in a way I never could have imagined. They fill me with more joy and happiness than I thought possible. Whether my time with the boys is encouraging or discouraging, my love for them grows stronger and stronger every day.

I love when my boys cuddle up next to me on the couch, when they laugh, or when they tell me their funny stories. They can throw their toys across the room in anger, drag dirt over my freshly cleaned carpet, or tell me they are mad at me; although it may be upsetting or frustrating, my heart is still theirs. I will always be there for them, guide them, and encourage them no matter what they do or say. I will forever love and cherish them. Nothing can change that. I know you feel the same way about your children.

How amazing it is that our Lord loves each of us with this same unconditional love. Just as we look adoringly at our children and smile, I believe he looks down on us from his heavenly throne with delight and adoration. It doesn't matter if we are doing everything right or if we are making mistakes, he loves us with all his almighty and powerful heart. Like our children, our actions may anger or displease our Father, but nothing can separate us from his love. He will always be there for us, teaching us, comforting us, and advising us. Is there any greater love than that?

God loves you so much. When times get challenging, he loves you. When you mess up, he loves you. When you celebrate a victory, he loves you. When you experience defeat, he loves you. If you are young or if you are old, he loves you. God has and will always love you, no matter what!

As you spend time with God today, reflect on the deep love you have for your children and rejoice over the deeper love God has for you!

> For I am convinced that neither death, nor life, nor angels, nor principalities, nor things present, nor things to come, nor powers, nor height, nor depth, nor any other created thing, will be able to separate us from the love of God, which is in Christ Jesus our Lord.
>
> Romans 8:38–39 (NASB)

## Take Just a Minute

# I Will Fight the Giant

When Clay was three, his preschool teacher read the story of David and Goliath. She read the verses where Goliath invited the Israelites to send a man to fight him for their freedom. Immediately, Clay exclaimed, "I will fight the giant!" He did not hesitate. He heard the request and he acted. Clay had no idea how tall or strong this Philistine was supposed to be, but he didn't care. He had faith and confidence. He believed in himself and his ability to conquer this giant. He was fearless.

If you are like me, you face many fears and obstacles on a regular basis. Financial stress, discipline issues, medical concerns, general management of the home, marital woes—all of these, at times, seem impossible to manage. We think too much, we worry too much, we doubt too much. We lack the faith and the confidence that comes so naturally to our children. Rather than facing our fears and concerns, we often hide from them, hoping they will go away. We feel alone. We are afraid.

Unfortunately, the hurdles you face won't just go away. They will linger and grow stronger the longer you hide. But let me encourage you. You can face your battles and you can win! You are not alone.

Just as God helped David fight his giant, our Lord and Savior is ready and willing to help you fight yours. When you have doubts and are weak, God can give you assurance and strength. When your faith is small, God can increase it. As you seek God, not only will he guide you and support you, but he can lead you to people and places who will offer you wisdom, direction, and encouragement. There is no battle too big or too small for God.

Spend time today thinking and praying about the battles you are facing. Pour out your heart to our Lord. Ask him for help. He is listening. You can have the faith and confidence of a little child. You can overcome. God is ready to fight the giants in your life! Are you ready to fight with him?

> And David said, "The Lord who delivered me from the paw of the lion and from the paw of the bear, He will deliver me from the hand of this Philistine." And Saul said to David, "Go, and may the Lord be with you."
>
> 1 Samuel 17:37 (NASB)

> Finally, be strong in the Lord and in the strength of His might.
>
> Ephesians 6:10 (NASB)

# Take Just a Minute

# A Minute for You

I have truly enjoyed sharing a collection of my favorite motherhood experiences with you. I hope you found comfort, wisdom, encouragement, and even a little laughter. Most importantly, I hope you have grown closer in your walk with our precious Lord and Savior, Jesus Christ.

Now that my story time is over, I hope you will take a few moments to write your own story. What has raising children taught you about yourself, your children, and about our Lord? Is there a scripture you often turn to when you need guidance or strength? How has prayer impacted your life? What advice would you like to share with other moms? What advice do you need?

As you reflect on your motherhood experiences, I hope you realize how much God loves you. I pray you will seek him daily. God is always there for you. May he continue to guide you and bless you through the joys and the challenges of motherhood.

> Seek the Lord and His strength; Seek His face continually.
>
> 1 Chronicles 16:11 (NASB)

Therefore encourage one another and build up one another, just as you also are doing.

1 Thessalonians 5:11 (NASB)

## Take Just a Minute

# They Make Me Smile Journal

As you read the daily devotional stories, I am sure you recalled special moments in your child's life that made you smile. Please use this section to capture those moments and any future moments that are sure to occur. I know you will enjoy sharing these entries with your children when they are older. What a wonderful time of joy and laughter you are sure to experience. I encourage you to continue journaling the moments that make you smile long after the pages in this section are full.

> Every good and perfect gift is from above, coming down from the father of the heavenly lights, who does not change like shifting shadows.
>
> James 1:17 (NIV)

He called a little child and had him stand among them. And he said: "I tell you the truth, unless you change and become like little children, you will never enter the kingdom of heaven. Therefore, whoever humbles himself like this child is the greatest in the kingdom of heaven."

Matthew 18:2–4 (NIV)

# They Make Me Smile

    Date            Moment that made you smile

♥ _____  _____

_____

_____

_____

_____

♥ _____  _____

_____

_____

_____

_____

✍ _____     _____

_____

_____

_____

✍ _____     _____

_____

_____

_____

✍ _____     _____

_____

_____

_____

✍ _____     _____

_____

_____

Train a child in the way he should go, and when he is old he will not turn from it.

Proverbs 22:6 (NIV)

I will give thanks to You, for I am fearfully and wonderfully made; wonderful are Your works, and my soul knows it very well.

Psalm 139:14 (NASB)

✒ _____    _____

✒ _____    _____

✒ _____    _____

✒ _____    _____

> Train a child in the way he should go, and when he is old he will not turn from it.
>
> Proverbs 22:6 (NIV)

♥ _____    _____

_____

_____

_____

♥ _____    _____

_____

_____

_____

♥ _____    _____

_____

_____

_____

♥ _____    _____

_____

_____

> I will give thanks to You, for I am fearfully and wonderfully made; wonderful are Your works, and my soul knows it very well.
>
> Psalm 139:14 (NASB)

♡ _____     _____

♡ _____     _____

♡ _____     _____

♡ _____     _____

> Train a child in the way he should go, and when he is old he will not turn from it.
>
> Proverbs 22:6 (NIV)

I will give thanks to You, for I am fearfully and wonderfully made; wonderful are Your works, and my soul knows it very well.

Psalm 139:14 (NASB)

✍ _____    _____

_____

_____

_____

✍ _____    _____

_____

_____

_____

✍ _____    _____

_____

_____

_____

✍ _____    _____

_____

_____

> Train a child in the way he should go, and when he is old he will not turn from it.
>
> Proverbs 22:6 (NIV)

ℒ❤ _____   _____
_____
_____
_____

ℒ❤ _____   _____
_____
_____
_____

ℒ❤ _____   _____
_____
_____
_____

ℒ❤ _____   _____
_____
_____

> I will give thanks to You, for I am fearfully and wonderfully made; wonderful are Your works, and my soul knows it very well.
>
> Psalm 139:14 (NASB)

Train a child in the way he should go, and when he is old he will not turn from it.

Proverbs 22:6 (NIV)

ℒ♥ _____  _____

_____

_____

_____

ℒ♥ _____  _____

_____

_____

_____

ℒ♥ _____  _____

_____

_____

_____

ℒ♥ _____  _____

_____

_____

> I will give thanks to You, for I am fearfully and wonderfully made; wonderful are Your works, and my soul knows it very well.
>
> Psalm 139:14 (NASB)

♌ _____    _____

♌ _____    _____

♌ _____    _____

♌ _____    _____

Train a child in the way he should go, and when he is old he will not turn from it.

Proverbs 22:6 (NIV)

I will give thanks to You, for I am fearfully and wonderfully made; wonderful are Your works, and my soul knows it very well.

Psalm 139:14 (NASB)

# Prayer and Praises to Our Lord Journal

Prayer is absolutely essential to a mother's life. Please use the following pages to enter prayer requests and praises as they relate to raising your children. I want to encourage you to take time to review these request and indicate when and how your prayers were answered. I know you will be blessed as you see God's faithfulness in your life and in the lives of your children.

> Rejoice evermore. Pray without ceasing. In every thing give thanks: for this is the will of God in Christ Jesus concerning you.
>
> 1 Thessalonians 5:16–18 (kjv)

> Therefore confess your sins to each other and pray for each other so that you may be healed. The prayer of a righteous man is powerful and effective.
>
> James 5:16 (niv)

Trust in the Lord with all your heart and do not lean on your own understanding. In all your ways acknowledge Him, and He will make your paths straight.

                              Proverbs 3:5–6 (NASB)

# Prayer and Praises to Our Lord

Date          Prayer Request or Praise

✎ _____    _____

_____

_____

_____

_____

✎ _____    _____

_____

_____

_____

_____

"For I know the plans I have for you, declares the Lord, plans to prosper you and not to harm you, plans to give you hope and a future."

Jeremiah 29:11 (NIV)

Humble yourselves, therefore, under God's mighty hand, that he may lift you up in due time. Cast all your anxiety on him because he cares for you.

1 Peter 5:6–7 (NIV)

"For I know the plans I have for you, declares the Lord, plans to prosper you and not to harm you, plans to give you hope and a future."

Jeremiah 29:11 (NIV)

✒ _____    _____










✒ _____    _____










✒ _____    _____










✒ _____    _____





> Humble yourselves, therefore, under God's mighty hand, that he may lift you up in due time. Cast all your anxiety on him because he cares for you.
>
> 1 Peter 5:6–7 (NIV)

"For I know the plans I have for you, declares the Lord, plans to prosper you and not to harm you, plans to give you hope and a future."

Jeremiah 29:11 (NIV)

✐ _____    _____

_____

_____

_____

✐ _____    _____

_____

_____

_____

✐ _____    _____

_____

_____

_____

✐ _____    _____

_____

_____

> Humble yourselves, therefore, under God's mighty hand, that he may lift you up in due time. Cast all your anxiety on him because he cares for you.
>
> 1 Peter 5:6–7 (NIV)

"For I know the plans I have for you, declares the Lord, plans to prosper you and not to harm you, plans to give you hope and a future."

Jeremiah 29:11 (NIV)

> Humble yourselves, therefore, under God's mighty hand, that he may lift you up in due time. Cast all your anxiety on him because he cares for you.
>
> 1 Peter 5:6–7 (NIV)

🍃 _____    _____

_____

_____

_____

🍃 _____    _____

_____

_____

_____

🍃 _____    _____

_____

_____

_____

🍃 _____    _____

_____

_____

_____

> "For I know the plans I have for you, declares the Lord, plans to prosper you and not to harm you, plans to give you hope and a future."
>
> Jeremiah 29:11 (NIV)

❦ _____    _____

_____

_____

_____

❦ _____    _____

_____

_____

_____

❦ _____    _____

_____

_____

_____

❦ _____    _____

_____

_____

> Humble yourselves, therefore, under God's mighty hand, that he may lift you up in due time. Cast all your anxiety on him because he cares for you.
>
> 1 Peter 5:6–7 (NIV)

"For I know the plans I have for you, declares the Lord, plans to prosper you and not to harm you, plans to give you hope and a future."

Jeremiah 29:11 (NIV)

> Humble yourselves, therefore, under God's mighty hand, that he may lift you up in due time. Cast all your anxiety on him because he cares for you.
>
> 1 Peter 5:6–7 (NIV)

# Final Thoughts

Thank you for reading *a Minute for Mommy*. I hope the daily devotionals encouraged you and helped you realize you are not alone on your motherhood journey. I also hope you enjoyed writing in the two journal sections.

I cannot end this book without asking you to think about your personal relationship with our Lord and Savior. I pray you know him, but if you don't know the Lord, or if you have questions about Jesus or what it means to have a personal relationship with him, I hope you will find a close friend or pastor to talk to soon. The Bible says, "I am the way and the truth and the life. No one comes to the father except through me" (John 14:6, NIV). It also says, "For God so loved the world that he gave his one and only Son, that whoever believes in him shall not perish but have eternal life" (John 3:16, NIV). There is no greater friend, comforter, and redeemer than Jesus Christ. He loves you so very much and desires a relationship with you deeper than any you have ever known.

Thank you for taking just a minute to draw yourself closer to your children and to the Lord. I hope you will continue to reflect on the blessings of motherhood and capture these special moments for many years to come.

> "For I know the plans I have for you," declares the Lord, "plans to prosper you and not to harm you, plans to give you hope and a future."
>
> Jeremiah 29:11 (NIV)